FAST FORWARD

Wild West

illustrated by

Mark Stacey

BARRON'S

Contents

Introduction

Imagine you are in the western United States, and it's hundreds of years ago. It is a vast, empty land, with nothing but grassy plains and herds of grazing buffalo. It may not seem very likely, but there is an exciting story to tell about what will happen here in the future. The events take many years to unfold, but you can follow them in this book.

The story is like a journey. It is not a journey you can make by plane, car or ship. In fact, you don't have to *go* anywhere at all. You are about to travel through time. With each turn of the page, the date moves forward a few years. You are still in the same place, but notice how many things change from one page to the next. Each date—each stop on your journey—is like a new chapter.

The time when the Indians had the land to themselves, the arrival of new settlers from overseas, the building of farms, villages and towns, the coming of the railroad, the days of cowboys, outlaws and gunfights—all tell the story of what has become known as the Wild West.

Use this thumb index to travel though time! Just find the page you want to see and flip it open. This way you can make a quick comparison between one scene and another, even though they show events that took place some years apart. A little black arrow on the page points to the date of the scene illustrated on that page.

The year AD 600

American Indians have lived on the Great Plains for thousands of years. They travel about on foot, hunting the herds of buffalo that roam the Plains. Buffalo provide the Indians with most of their food. Their skins, fur and bones are useful for making clothes, teepees (tents), weapons and tools.

As soon the lookouts spot a herd of buffalo, the hunters begin to stalk them. Carefully herding the animals along valleys, they slowly drive them toward a strong wooden enclosure, called a corral, which they have already built.

buffalo meat onto a wooden rack to dry. This will be the main food supply for the group when the buffalo have moved on.

The children of the camp run about and play, but there is also work to be done. Girls help their mothers, while boys learn how to use weapons.

Inside a teepee, one of the elders of the group tells stories to the children to teach them about the tribe's history. The teepee has warm hides on the floor and wooden backrests to lean against.

ravois

Chief

Backrest

The 1840s

A group of white settlers from far away in the East are traveling across the Plains in search of new, fertile farm land in the West. The settlers travel in wagons drawn by mules, horses or oxen. As evening falls, they draw their wagons

Looking at maps

Buffalo chips

Repairing a wagon wheel

into a circle to keep out wild animals.

The men repair their wagons, feed the animals and consult maps to plan for the next day's travel. The children play while women prepare the evening meal over a fire of buffalo dung or "buffalo chips". They rely on the food stores they carry, as food is scarce on the Plains.

Indians

Wagon

A few years later ...

A group of families from the East are traveling westwards toward Oregon or California. They have been inspired by reports from previous travelers, who tell of rich farmland and a pleasant climate. On their journey west, however, the group have met other travelers who have given up and turned back. They warn the families to expect hardships such as hunger, thirst, heat and cold. Deadly diseases such as cholera are common, and have killed many people.

The group hope they will have more luck. One of their fears, however, is attack by fierce Indian tribes. But the Indians they meet are friendly and eager to trade goods, although some demand money for passing through their lands.

Trading blankets

Buffalo hides

Trading guns

By now, the Indians are used to white settlers. They have traded with fur trappers and adventurers—known as "mountain men"—for many years.

As the wagon train pauses to rest, the Indians trade buffalo hides and dried buffalo meat for blankets, guns and luxuries such as beads and mirrors. They also help the travelers to plan the next part of their route.

THE GOLD RUSH

Not all travelers along the Oregon or California Trails were in search of fertile farmland. The Mormons, a group following the teachings of Joseph Smith, left the East where they were hated and attacked for their beliefs. They settled on the deserted shores of the Great Salt Lake in Utah.

In 1848 gold was discovered in California. Tens of thousands of men went there in the hope of making a fortune to take home to the East, but few actually did. Towns grew up around mining areas. Although many were quickly deserted when the gold ran out, some eventually became large cities.

AD 600

1800

A few years later

The 1840s

A few years later

Planning a route

15

The 1860s

Settlers are now setting up home on the Great Plains. They come not only from the eastern states but also from abroad. This family has come from Eastern Europe. They have almost finished building their farm, or homestead.

With little wood to be found on the Plains, their house is built from sod, slabs of turf cut from the ground. The heavy ground is baked hard by the sun and difficult to cut, so the family must wait until it has been softened by rain. Special heavy plows are needed to prepare the ground for sowing crops.

Collecting buffalo dung

Cutting sod

The women look after the family and cook the meals. They collect dried buffalo dung to fuel the fires and antlers that will later be ground down into fertilizer for the crops. The nearest homestead is miles away, so visitors are always welcome.

LAND FOR FREE

To encourage people to settle on the Plains, the U.S. Government passed the Homestead Act of 1862. This set aside large areas of land, and gave people a plot of 160 acres for free as long as they built a house and lived there for five years. Hundreds of thousands of settlers eagerly took up this opportunity.

Among the new settlers were black people who had once been slaves, but were now free. They were now able to build their own homes and farms.

AD 600

1800

A few years later

The 1840s

A few years later

The 1860s

A few years later

Grass fire

Sod house

Buffalo dung

Antlers

Plowing

17

The first ranchers settled on the Texas prairies. They used cowboys to herd their cattle north across the Great Plains to the railroads, to be transported to markets in the East. Later ranchers set up home on the Great Plains, closer to the railroads.

Early ranches were unfenced and cattle could wander for miles. The invention of barbed wire fencing meant that ranchers could keep their own cattle on their land and wild cattle out.

Route of new railroad

Windmill

On the bare, dry Plains, many farms and towns used windmills to pump water up from under the ground. In railroad towns these were especially important to provide water for the steam engines of the trains.

Tents

Wagon

Church

TAILORS SHOP

PUBLIC SCHOOL

Stagecoach

Photographer

In a few more years ...

The site where the homestead used to stand has now grown into a small town. A new railroad is being built, which will pass by the town, carrying goods and cattle. People have come here to set up homes and businesses.

Many of the buildings in the small town are only temporary shacks or tents, homes to the men who are working to build the railroad. There are also more permanent wooden buildings, such as a church and a saloon. A small school has been built for the children of the few families living in the town.

As the railroad workers haul the rails into place, other men are building barbed wire fences to make cattle pens. Telegraph poles are being erected next to the railroad, so that messages can be passed from one end of the country to the other. A stagecoach is being loaded with passengers' baggage and mail. Until the railroad is completed, the stagecoach is the fastest way to travel.

AD 600

1800

A few years later

The 1840s

A few years later

The 1860s

A few years later

In a few more years

Building fences

Telegraph pole

Supervisor

Building railroad tracks

The 1870s

The small town has grown rapidly since the railroad was completed. Wood has been brought in by rail to build more houses, as well as shops and hotels. There are wooden walkways outside the buildings on the main streets. In front of the walkways are wooden hitching rails for people to tie up their horses.

Busy cattle towns often attracted criminals, known as outlaws. Cattle rustlers tried to steal cattle as cowboys drove the cattle toward the town. Other outlaws were robbers, highway-men or even murderers. Some outlaws, such as Billy the Kid and Jesse James, became well known. People wrote stories about their adventures, and myths grew up about how they lived and died.

New church

GENERAL STORE

METROPOLITAN HOTEL

LEE & HI

BEATY & KELLY

Stagecoach

Lucky ST
SAL

Hitching rail

Wooden sidewalks

Cattle

The town plays an important part in the cattle trade. Cowboys drive cattle from ranches in the South across the Plains to the town. They herd the cattle into pens and then load them onto trains headed for markets in the East.

When the cattle are loaded, the cowboys can enjoy life in town. There are plenty of boarding houses to stay in, and saloons, bars and dance halls for them to relax in after weeks or even months on the cattle trails.

Old church

Telegraph wires

Herding cattle onto train

Cattle pens

Steam train

ELITE LODGINGS

Stables

LIVERY

Cowboys

AD 600

1800

A few years later

The 1840s

A few years later

The 1860s

A few years later

In a few more years

The 1870s

A few years later ...

The town is even bigger, and has become quite rowdy. Outlaws come into town to steal horses, and to rob people. The cowboys that throng the town also cause a lot of trouble. They spend most of the money they have earned from the cattle drive on drinking and gambling, which often causes arguments and fighting.

There were several kinds of law officers. Local marshals *(above)* made sure that their towns were law-abiding, and dealt with minor crimes such as fights. Sheriffs were in charge of counties. Both sheriffs and marshals had deputies to help them, and also used groups, or posses of local people when hunting an outlaw. U.S. marshals and their deputies took charge of a territory or state. They dealt with those accused of more serious crimes, and brought them to court to face a judge.

Saloon and boarding house

Jail

STORE

Grocery store

Marshal

Posse

In the saloon, a drunken fight has started because someone has cheated in a card game. In the street outside, passers-by run for cover as a gunfight breaks out. The marshal hurries out of the jail to break up the fight before too many people get hurt.

LAW AND ORDER

At first, nobody took charge of law and order in the new towns that grew up across the West. Instead local people, called vigilantes, grouped together to catch outlaws and hang them for their crimes. However, the vigilantes also attacked innocent people and their own personal enemies.

As the towns grew, and families began to move into them, the U.S. government sent in marshals, sheriffs and judges. These lawmen often helped to "clean up" a town—but some were criminals themselves.

Hotel and saloon

Stables

Gunfight

AD 600

1800

A few years later

The 1840s

A few years later

The 1860s

A few years later

In a few more years

The 1870s

A few years later

Early 1900s

Today

On the outskirts of a modern city, with its towering skyscrapers and fast pace of life, a Wild West theme park has been built. It has thrilling rides such as rollercoasters, and there are many shows and attractions. People dressed as cowboys ride up and down the streets. A crowd gathers to watch a show where a shootout takes place. The actors make this seem funny and exciting.

Mock hanging

Cavalry parade

Stagecoach

Cowboy skills

Pony rides

A rodeo show demonstrates real-life cowboy skills such as bull roping and riding. Children can go for rides on a pony, in a stagecoach or even on a miniature railroad. There are many fast food restaurants, and a saloon with music and dancing girls.

Visitors come from miles around to experience a little of the Wild West, but does this match real life in the Wild West a century ago?

Skyscrapers

Rollercoaster

Miniature railroad

Shootout show

AD 600

1800

A few years later

The 1840s

A few years later

The 1860s

A few years later

In a few more years

The 1870s

A few years later

Early 1900s

Today

Glossary

Cattle trail The route taken by cowboys driving herds of cattle. There were several main cattle trails, including the trail north from Texas to towns on the railroad.

Cavalry A group of soldiers that fought on horseback.

Corral A pen for cattle, or for buffalo herded together for slaughter. A defensive circle of wagons made by white settlers was also called a corral.

Cowboys Men who rounded up and drove cattle along cattle trails. Some were white laborers from the east. Others were black former slaves or Indians.

Deputy Second-in-command to a marshal or sheriff.

Great Plains A vast tract of land in North America lying between the Mississippi River to the east and the Rocky Mountains to the west. Before white people settled there, the Plains were barren grasslands grazed by buffalo and inhabited by a number of different Indian tribes.

Homestead A farm established by settlers on the Great Plains. Encouraged by the offer of cheap land from the U.S. Government, "homesteaders" first moved onto the Plains in the 1860s.

Marshal A U.S. marshal was appointed by the U.S. Government. He was responsible for bringing to justice people suspected of serious crimes, like robbing a train. A town marshal dealt with minor matters such as fights and brawls.

Nickelodeon An early cinema or movie theater. The entrance charge was five cents.

Outlaw Someone who led a life of crime, often robbing banks and trains for money and valuables.

Posse A group of men called on by a town marshal or sheriff to hunt down an outlaw.

Ranch A large farm on the Great Plains where people known as ranchers raised cattle.

Reservations Areas where Indian tribes were forced to live by the U.S. Government. They were made to give up their traditional way of life.

Rodeo A round-up of cattle, or an exhibition of cowboy skills.

Sheriff A law officer appointed by a county. He was like a local policeman.

Stagecoach A carriage, usually pulled by six horses, that carried passengers and mail across the West. It made regular stops, known as "stages", on the way.

Teepee A large cone-shaped tent made of buffalo hides hung on poles. Most Plains Indians lived in villages made up of teepees.

Telegraph The sending of messages by electrical signals along wires.

Travois A horse-drawn sled used by the Indians to transport their teepees and belongings.

Vigilantes A group of people who took charge of law and order for themselves.